FACT * OR FAKE ?

THE TRUTH ABOUT
DINOSAURS

SONYA NEWLAND

First published in Great Britain in 2022 by Wayland
Copyright © Hodder and Stoughton Limited, 2022

Produced for Wayland by
White-Thomson Publishing Ltd
www.wtpub.co.uk

All rights reserved.

Editor: Sonya Newland
Series Designer: Rocket Design (East Anglia) Ltd
Designer: Clare Nicholas
Consultant: Steve Parker

HB ISBN: 978 1 5263 1852 7
PB ISBN: 978 1 5263 1853 4

Wayland
An imprint of
Hachette Children's Group
Part of Hodder & Stoughton
Carmelite House
50 Victoria Embankment
London EC4Y 0DZ

An Hachette UK Company

www.hachettechildrens.co.uk

Printed in China

Picture acknowledgements:
Shutterstock: Ron Leishman 4, dedMazay 5, 42, 60, Ken Benner 6, Kolia_stock 6–7, Planet Urf 7, 58, 62, Studio Ayutaka 8, Chereliss 9, oixxo 10, 11, Adam Studio 75 12, Teguh Mujiono 13t, T_Dub0v 13b, Vector Tradition 14, Gular Samadova 15t, JocularityArt 15b, stockakia 16, Sararoom Design 17, 44, 87, DINOONCAM 19, Vorobiov Oleksii 8 20, julio chaniago 76 21l, VladisChern 21r, CartoonDesignerFX 22, rivansyam 23a, Arcady 23b, Julinzy 24, shaineast 25, Christos Georghiou 26, RVV-DESIGN 27, Mokool Graphics 28a, jame05 28b, Visual Generation 28c, owatta 29, 34a, Elfhame 30, Emil Mammadov 31, ledokolua 32, Kristyna Vagnerova 33, Drawlab19 34b, MaxNadya 35a, Mivta Design 35b, SimpLine 36, klerik78 37, Motimo 38, SINGINK 39, LA54, 9 40, ria_airborne 41, Robert Adrian Hillman 43, lady-luck 45, Memo Angeles 46, Far700 48, Olor688 49, Svitalsky 50, shuttersport 51, nickolai_self_taught 52, Teguh Mujiono 53, scworkspace vector art 55, Doddy Picture 56, Yayayoyo 57, sollalexta 59, Vector Micro Master 61, Olo_lo 63, scworkspace vector art 64–65, Klara Viskova 66, The Crafty Clip 67, lineartestpilot 68, mspoint 69, smirinika 70, joker140226 71, Dian Elvina 72t, Fir4ik 72m, Zaie 72b, anak tinta 73, CitraDesignPro 74, 78, Phakorn Kasikij 75, Morphart Creation 76, Li Bro 77, robodread 79, Tony Oshlick 80, Artur Balytskyi 81, ledokolua 82, Erik D 83, BNP Design Studio 84, AprintStore 85, Damien Che 86t, Oleksii Arseniuk 86b, Ain Mikail 88, Good_Stock 89, Ron Leishman 90–91.

All design elements from Shutterstock.

Every effort has been made to clear copyright. Should there be any inadvertent omission, please apply to the publisher for rectification.

The website addresses (URLs) included in this book were valid at the time of going to press. However, it is possible that contents or addresses may have changed since the publication of this book. No responsibility for any such changes can be accepted by either the author or the publisher.

All facts and statistics were correct at the time of press, but new information is always being discovered about dinosaurs, and facts may change.

CAN YOU SEPARATE THE FACTS FROM THE FAKES?

STEGOSAURUS HAD TWO BRAINS.

NO WAY!

THERE'S A DINOSAUR NAMED AFTER HOGWARTS SCHOOL.

YOU'RE JOKING!

T. REX STOOD UPRIGHT.

DUH, EVERYONE KNOWS THAT!

DINOSAURS WERE GREAT PARENTS.

NOT LIKELY ...

Read on to find out the reality behind popular myths and mind-blowing truths about dinosaurs. Discover the science behind the facts and then dazzle your friends and family with amazing, bizarre — and sometimes downright unbelievable — facts about these prehistoric creatures.

'DINOSAUR' MEANS 'TERRIBLE LIZARD'

I'm not so terrible!

FACT OR FAKE?

If you'd used the word 'dinosaur' before 1842, no one would have known what you were on about. That was the year that scientist Richard Owen coined the term 'Dinosauria' to describe the creatures whose fossils had recently been discovered.

THE SCIENCE

Although the word is now translated as 'terrible lizard', Owen's exact description was 'fearfully great reptiles'. It was intended to reflect their enormous size more than how scary they were – although they were, of course, terrifying!

FIRST FOSSILS

When the word dinosaur was first used, only three kinds were known from fossil finds: *Megalosaurus*, *Iguanodon* and *Hylaeosaurus*.

VERDICT

Fact

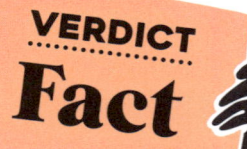

ARCHAEOLOGISTS DIG UP DINOSAURS

Ooo, dino bones?!

FACT OR FAKE?

An archaeologist might stumble across a dinosaur fossil by chance, but scientifically speaking, an archaeologist is someone who studies *human* history. Palaeontologists are the people who study fossilised forms of all past life, including dinosaurs!

THE SCIENCE

Palaeontology is the study of ancient animals and plants. Palaeontologists work all over the world, digging up and analysing fossils. These remains of ancient living things reveal the secrets of life on our planet millions of years ago. They can show how Earth changed in the past – and even hint at what lies in its future!

VERDICT

Fake

DINOSAURS LIVED FOR

Dinosaurs were around for a LONG time! All in all, they roamed the planet for around 165 million years, before being wiped out by what scientists refer to as an 'extinction event', about 66 million years ago.

TRIASSIC
(252–201 million years ago)

JURASSIC
(201–145 million years ago)

HUMAN HISTORY
Compared to the length of time that dinosaurs ruled Earth, humans have been here for just a blink of the eye — a mere 200,000 years!

165 MILLION YEARS

What are you?

CRETACEOUS
(145–66 million years ago)

THE SCIENCE

The age of dinosaurs is split into three periods: the Triassic, the Jurassic and the Cretaceous. Together these are known as the Mesozoic Era. Different species of dinosaur didn't all exist for this whole time – some species were separated by millions of years!

VERDICT
Fact

LL DINOSAURS WERE REPTILES

We're one big happy family ...

The Mesozoic Era is also known as the 'Age of Reptiles', so that's a clue right there. Although there were other types of animal on Earth at the time, most large land creatures were reptiles, including all the animals that scientists classify as dinosaurs.

THE SCIENCE

Reptiles are a large group, or class, of animals that share common features. They all have four legs and a backbone, and most reptiles lay eggs. Animals in the same class are also linked to a common ancestor. So, dinosaurs match the definition of reptiles.

CLASSIFYING CREATURES

All living things are classified by a scientific name. You're a *Homo sapiens* ('wise human'). A *Tyrannosaurus rex* is, well, a *Tyrannosaurus rex* ('king of the tyrant lizards')!

VERDICT
Fact

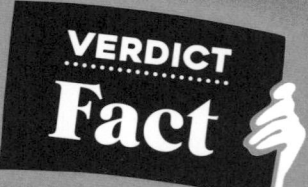

TRICERATOPS HAD THREE HORNS

FACT OR FAKE?

The name *Triceratops* comes from the Greek *tri* (three), *keras* (horn) and *ops* (face), so it would have been strange if it had one, two or four horns! *Triceratops* had two huge 'brow' horns above its eyes and a smaller horn on its snout.

THE SCIENCE

On young *Triceratops*, the brow horns were stubby and curved backwards. As the animal grew, the horns got bigger and straighter. By the time it reached adulthood – when the *Triceratops* was about the size of an African elephant – these deadly weapons were about 1 m long! *Triceratops* probably used their horns when fighting each other or defending themselves from attack.

VERDICT

Fact

ALL DINOSAURS

Hey Grandpa!

FACT OR FAKE?

People used to think that all dinosaurs died out around 66 million years ago. But experts have proved that birds evolved from small, meat-eating dinosaurs. So birds are a sub-group of dinosaurs and, since birds are alive, they are living dinosaurs!

THE SCIENCE

The latest evidence shows that small, meat-eating dinosaurs called maniraptorans evolved into the first birds. So most scientists now say that the dinosaur group lives on as birds. However the huge, fearsome, scaly dinosaurs are certainly all gone. Those are usually now called non-bird or non-avian dinosaurs.

VERDICT
Fake

ARE EXTINCT

BIRD? DINOSAUR? BOTH?

When the 150-million-year-old fossils of *Archaeopteryx* were discovered, they were thought to belong to a dinosaur. Then scientists decided they were from the earliest bird. Today, birds are regarded as living dinosaurs, so *Archaeopteryx* is both!

DINOSAURS WERE ALL HUGE CREATURES

FACT OR FAKE?

There were certainly some MASSIVE dinosaurs – some of the sauropods were the biggest creatures ever to walk Earth. But dinosaurs came in all different sizes, some of them no bigger than a chicken!

THE SCIENCE

One of the smallest known dinosaurs was tiny *Parvicursor*. These little reptiles belonged to the group of maniraptoran theropods that evolved into birds (see pages 10–11). They were less than 40 cm long and weighed about half as much as this book!

VERDICT
....
Fake

THE CLAW
Each of *Parvicursor*'s hands was basically one single claw. They probably used it for breaking into termite mounds to find food.

MEGALOSAURUS
WAS THE FIRST
DINOSAUR TO BE NAMED

It's quite an honour to be the first dinosaur – or at least the first one that fossil hunters gave a name to. Later, when loads more species were discovered, experts got creative with their names. But the name they came up with for the first one was *Megalosaurus* – 'great lizard'.

THE SCIENCE

A *Megalosaurus* bone was discovered in England in 1676. People suggested that the bone belonged to a giant elephant – or even a giant human. It wasn't until much later that people realised it belonged to an unknown type of animal. In 1824, the British scientist William Buckland said it came from an extinct giant reptile, which he called *Megalosaurus*.

Get me out of here!

VERDICT
Fact

13

WHEN **DINOSAURS** FIRST EVOLVED, EARTH HAD ONE GIANT CONTINENT

FACT OR FAKE?

Millions and millions of years ago, the surface of our planet looked very different from the way it does today. There weren't lots of landmasses separated by sea. In the early Triassic Period (see page 6), when dinosaurs evolved, there was just one huge landmass, which we now call Pangaea.

THE SCIENCE

This supercontinent slowly began to break apart about 175 million years ago, in the early Jurassic Period. The pieces spread around the globe, although it was many millions more years before they took the form of the continents that we're familiar with today.

VERDICT
Fact

DIPLODOCUS'S

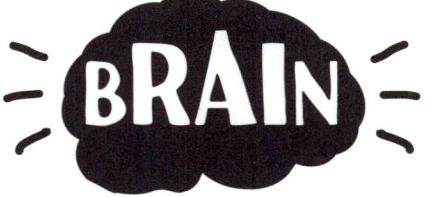

BRAIN

WAS THE SIZE OF A WALNUT

FACT OR FAKE?

Diplodocus is a famously dim dinosaur! Despite its massive body, it had a very small head. And a head that small could only contain a tiny brain. But did a beast bigger than a bus *really* have a brain only the size of a walnut? Not quite.

THE SCIENCE

Experts can work out roughly how big a dinosaur's brain was from the size of the brain case in the skull. *Diplodocus*'s brain is thought to have weighed about 110 g. That's more than a walnut, but still small. Your brain weighs more than ten times that!

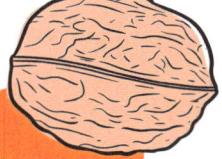

BRAIN FAIL

Diplodocus's unfortunate brain reputation comes from a writer called Jennie Irene Mix, who made the walnut comparison in her book *Mighty Animals* in 1912.

VERDICT
....
Fake

DINOSAURS WERE
COLD-BLOODED

FACT OR FAKE?

One commonly accepted feature of reptiles is that they are cold-blooded. In real terms that means they can't regulate their own body temperature – they have to use the environment to do that. For example, reptiles bask in the sunshine to get warm or move into the shade to cool down.

THE SCIENCE

The odd thing about dinosaurs is that although they're classified as reptiles (see page 8), scientists now think that some of them may not have been cold-blooded. Some may have been able to regulate their own body temperature after all, in the way that their living dinosaur descendants can – the birds.

Brrr!

VERDICT
Fake

TEMPERATURE TERMINOLOGY

If you want to sound like an animal expert, use the long words that scientists use. Warm-blooded animals (including you!) that can regulate their own body temperature are *endothermic*. Cold-blooded animals are *ectothermic*.

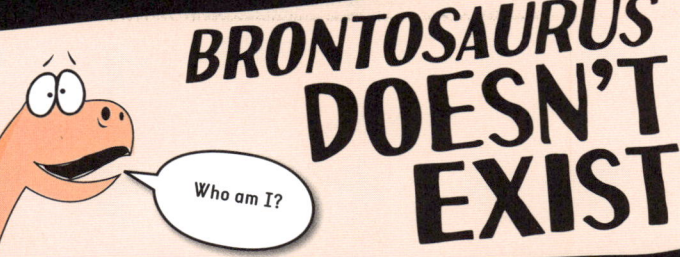

BRONTOSAURUS DOESN'T EXIST

Who am I?

Poor *Brontosaurus* has had an uncertain existence! Fossils of *Brontosaurus*, a member of the group of huge herbivores known as sauropods, were first discovered in the 1870s. But within a few years, people began wondering if these fossils were actually those of *Apatosaurus* ...

THE SCIENCE

For more than 100 years, *Brontosaurus* disappeared as an individual genus. But then in 2015, scientists discovered that it *was* different from *Apatosaurus* after all! And so the 'thunder lizard' came back into existence.

VERDICT

Fake

17

MOST DINOSAURS WERE GREYISH-GREEN

For a long time, scientists assumed that dinosaurs were pretty dull – at least in terms of colouring. They thought they were probably the same kind of green, grey or brown as reptiles such as crocodiles and many lizards. But the truth may be much more colourful!

THE SCIENCE

Animals come in all colours and patterns – bright and dull, spots and splodges, stripes and patches. So, why would a diverse group of creatures like the dinosaurs all be the same boring colour? Modern technology means that scientists are able to detect traces of pigment in fossils. These suggest that dinosaur skin or hair came in a variety of colours.

VERDICT
Fake

TYRANNOSAURUS
WAS THE BIGGEST MEAT-EATER

FACT OR FAKE?

Tyrannosaurus rex is probably the best-known dinosaur. We picture it as a huge, vicious predator, constantly on the hunt for other species to make its next meal. At about 13 m, *T. rex* was certainly a large land carnivore – but it wasn't the biggest. That record belongs to *Spinosaurus*.

THE SCIENCE

The 15-m-long, 10-tonne 'spine lizard' had a row of spines down its back, which were covered in and connected by skin, to create a kind of 'sail'. The spines themselves were more than 2 m long, making this dinosaur the most massive meat-eater.

FISH OR FLESH?
Despite its huge jaws, sharp teeth and scary spines, *Spinosaurus* may actually have preferred a diet of fish to feasting on land animals.

VERDICT
Fake

DINOSAURS ARE GROUPED BY THEIR HIPS

My hips don't lie!

FACT OR FAKE?

It might seem like an odd starting-place to classify a group of animals, but that's how scientists do it! All dinosaurs belong to one of two groups that are based on their hip structure. The Ornithischia are the 'bird-hipped' dinosaurs and the Saurischia are the 'lizard-hipped' dinosaurs.

THE SCIENCE

Each of these groups is sub-divided. The Saurischia include meat-eating theropods, such as *Tyrannosaurus*, and the huge sauropods, such as *Brachiosaurus*. Ornithiscia include the armoured thyreophorans, such as *Stegosaurus*, and unusual cerapods, such as *Triceratops*.

VERDICT

Fact

SOME BIG DINOSAURS COULD FLY

FACT OR FAKE?

You've probably seen pictures of huge flying creatures in prehistoric landscapes, so some dinosaurs must have been able to fly, right? Despite birds being living dinosaurs and some small dinosaurs probably being able to fly, the huge airborne animals of Mesozoic times weren't actually dinosaurs.

THE SCIENCE

However – don't be fooled into thinking that these animals were prehistoric birds. Flying creatures such as the pterosaurs were reptiles like the dinosaurs, but they were a distinct group, with different features and characteristics.

VERDICT

Fake

SHARED ANCESTORS

Pterosaurs and dinosaurs would have shared a common ancestor millions and millions of years earlier. But at some point the two groups split and started evolving in different ways.

DINOSAURS DRAGGED THEIR TAILS ALONG THE GROUND

FACT OR FAKE?

Think about the size of those huge, heavy tails – it would hardly be surprising if dinosaurs dragged them along the ground behind them. But despite their tails being huge and heavy, most dinosaurs walked with them lifted clear of the ground.

THE SCIENCE

All dinosaurs had tails. In bigger dinosaurs, such as sauropods, the tail was essential for balancing the weight of their huge body and long neck. Most dinosaurs had extremely strong thigh muscles to be able to lift and move their tail.

HOW DO WE KNOW?

If dinosaurs dragged their tails along the ground, we would have found imprints of this in the same places where footprints have been found.

VERDICT
....
Fake

VELOCIRAPTOR WAS THE MOST INTELLIGENT DINOSAUR

> I gots the smarts.

FACT OR FAKE?

Certain famous films have shown *Velociraptor* as a brainy dinosaur, able to plan in packs and outsmart humans. These carnivores may have been quite cunning in catching their prey, but most experts give the award for Most Intelligent Dinosaur to the small theropod *Troodon*.

THE SCIENCE

Compared to its body size, *Troodon* had a big brain – certainly relative to many other dinosaurs! Proportionally, its brain was bigger than those of most modern reptiles, so it might have been brainier than them, too.

VERDICT
Fake

IGUANODON HAD THUMBS

The huge herbivore *Iguanodon* has provided a puzzle for palaeontologists. On its front limbs it had a large 'thumb spike', opposite a little finger that stuck out to the side. No one knows exactly what this strange 'thumb' was for.

THE SCIENCE

When it was first discovered, experts thought this spike was part of *Iguanodon*'s snout – like a kind of horn. But when a more complete fossil skeleton was discovered later, they realised it went on the dinosaur's unusual hands.

VERDICT
Fact

SECOND PLACE
Iguanodon was the second dinosaur to be named, after *Megalosaurus* (see page 13). Its name means 'iguana tooth'.

24

See ya, kids!

DINOSAURS WERE UNCARING PARENTS

FACT OR FAKE?

All creatures have different parenting techniques. Some lay eggs then wander off, or abandon their young soon after birth and leave them to fend for themselves. Others – like humans – remain in family groups for life. So which category do dinosaurs belong to?

THE SCIENCE

For a long time, experts thought that dinosaurs didn't do much in the way of parenting. But there is now evidence that some species took good care of their young. *Maiasaura* ('good mother lizard'), for example, may have nurtured and fiercely protected its babies. Fossils have been found of adult *Maiasaura* with lots of young ones.

VERDICT
Fake

TYRANNOSAURUS
HAD SMALL, WEAK ARMS

FACT OR FAKE?

Compared to its large body, its big head and its muscular back legs, *Tyrannosaurus*'s arms do look oddly small. But don't get the idea that those little limbs were harmless!

THE SCIENCE

To start with, *Tyrannosaurus*'s arms only look small in relation to the rest of its body. Really, they were nearly 1 m long and more than three times as muscular as the arms of a strong human. They were perfectly useful for grabbing prey and holding it tight before the dinosaur used its terrifying jaws to chomp the prey to pieces …

VERDICT
Fake

BAMBIRAPTOR WAS NAMED AFTER THE DISNEY DEER

FACT OR FAKE?

Bambiraptor was a small, bird-like meat-eater, with wings and feathers. It got its name from the young deer in Disney's film *Bambi*, because the fossil skeleton that was found came from a juvenile of the species.

THE SCIENCE

This young dinosaur was discovered by someone equally young – a 14-year-old boy out fossil hunting with his parents! It turned out to be an enormously important find, as the skeleton was almost complete. This meant that palaeontologists could work out a lot of information about the species.

FICTIONAL NAMESAKES

Other dinosaurs named after fictional characters include *Zuul crurivastator* (the baddie in the film *Ghostbusters*) and *Gojirasaurus quayi* (named after Godzilla).

VERDICT

Fact

27

DINOSAURS WERE EITHER CARNIVORES OR HERBIVORES?

FACT OR FAKE?

You know about the fearsome flesh-eating theropods such as *Tyrannosaurus* and *Allosaurus*. And you know about the gentle, plant-eating giants such as *Brachiosaurus* and *Stegosaurus*. But not all dinosaurs stuck to a diet that was strictly meat or veg.

THE SCIENCE

A few dinosaurs (perhaps just 2 per cent of all species) were omnivores – that is, they ate both plants and other animals. They were usually opportunistic eaters, which means these dinosaurs ate whatever they got the chance to eat, whether that was a tasty plant or a passing mammal.

ANCIENT INSECTS

There were many insects around in prehistoric times – and they were a lot bigger than they are today. Many omnivores gobbled up a supersize scorpion or a massive millipede!

VERDICT

Fake

LARGE HERBIVORES ATE STONES

FACT OR FAKE?

In the stomach and rib cage of some dinosaurs, scientists have found collections of small stones, sometimes around 1 cm big. It wasn't that these beasts had just fancied rocks for dinner the day they died; the stones did an important job in terms of digestion.

THE SCIENCE

It seems that many plant-eating dinosaurs swallowed stones. The stones, known as gastroliths, helped to grind down the tough plant matter that the dinosaurs ate, so that it could be digested more easily. Some modern birds swallow small gastroliths, too.

Yum, stones!

VERDICT
....
Fact

29

DINOSAURS LAID EGGS

Can I come out now, Mum?

FACT OR FAKE?

One of the features of reptiles is that they lay eggs. Modern crocs, alligators and most lizards hatch from eggs. And so did the dinosaurs. How did a baby beast as big as *Argentinosaurus* fit in an egg, you ask? Well, some of the eggs were pretty big!

THE SCIENCE

Many dinosaurs laid their eggs in nests in the ground – some species laid more than 20 eggs at a time. Not many dinosaur eggs have been found, so it's hard to know how big they were for different species, but they probably ranged from tennis-ball size to half a metre long!

VERDICT
Fact

EGG PROTECTION
Dinosaurs probably covered the eggs in their nests with leaves to keep them warm.

THERE'S A DINOSAUR NAMED AFTER THE HARRY POTTER BOOKS

FACT OR FAKE?

Could there really be a *Harrius potterex* or a *Dumbledoropod*? Well, neither of those is a real dinosaur, but *Dracorex hogwartsia* is! The 'dragon king of Hogwarts' dinosaur was discovered in 2004.

THE SCIENCE

Dracorex got its name because of its skull, which looks a bit like how you'd imagine a dragon's head to look – all covered in knobs and spikes. It belongs to a group of dinosaurs called pachycephalosaurs, which had very bony heads, either thick and flat or shaped like a dome.

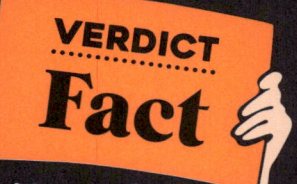

VERDICT

Fact

THERE WAS NO SUCH SPECIES AS PTERODACTYL

That's news to me!

FACT OR FAKE?

People often refer to a *Pterodactyl* as if it was a particular species of prehistoric creature, like *Tyrannosaurus rex*. In fact, it's not a species at all, but rather a commonly used name for a *group* of winged reptiles. And officially, this group is called Pterosauria, or pterosaurs.

THE SCIENCE

Generally speaking, scientists prefer to focus on the genera that make up the Pterosauria. Among these are *Pteranodon* and *Pterodactylus* (which is probably where the confusion arises!)

LORDS OF THE AIR

Pterosauria comprised two main subgroups: rhamphorhynchoids (or basal pterosaurs) and pterodactyloids. The basal pterosaurs had all died out by the end of the Jurassic Period, leaving the pterodactyloids to rule the prehistoric skies.

VERDICT
Fact

DINOSAURS HAD

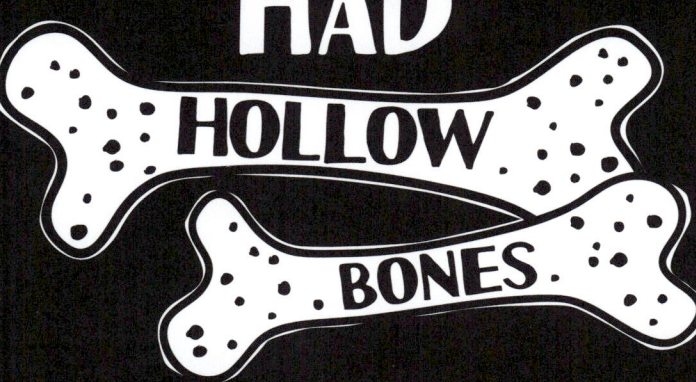

HOLLOW BONES

FACT OR FAKE?

For a long time, scientists studying dinosaurs and other prehistoric reptiles were puzzled by a big question. How did animals this big move so fast – and even take flight? It turned out that the answer was in their bones ...

THE SCIENCE

Solid bone is very heavy: any large creature carrying that amount of weight would struggle to move at speed. Some dinosaurs had hollows, or cavities, in their bones. These 'air sacs' vastly reduced the animals' weight and allowed them to move quickly.

VERDICT

Fact

DINOSAURS LIVED ON EVERY CONTINENT

FACT OR FAKE?

It's an amazing fact that dinosaur fossils have been found on every one of Earth's seven continents – including Antarctica. Although these ancient creatures lived all over the planet, some parts of the world have yielded many more fossils than others.

THE SCIENCE

The most fossils, and the greatest variety of species, have been found in desert areas in North America, China and Argentina. But this doesn't necessarily mean that more dinosaurs lived there, just that it's easier to find fossils where there are large, bare, rocky areas.

WARM ANTARCTICA

You might think that dinosaurs couldn't have survived in the frozen landscape of Antarctica. But in the Mesozoic Era, the polar regions were very different – covered in lush forests rather than ice.

VERDICT

Fact

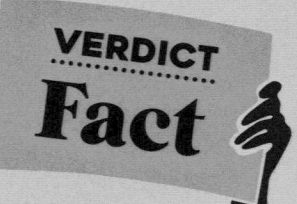

SAUROPODS LIVED IN SWAMPS

I'm going for a paddle.

FACT OR FAKE?

It's a common dinosaur myth that the biggest type of dinosaurs, the sauropods, inhabited swamps rather than spending too much time on solid ground. There, it was thought, they lived their lives partly in water, which helped support their bulky bodies.

THE SCIENCE

Today, scientists think differently. They're pretty sure that, despite the sauropods' size, most lived on land rather than in swamps. Their bodies aren't any better suited to swimming than they are to land-life. In fact, their strong hips and shoulders show that they were well able to support themselves on solid ground.

VERDICT

Fake

MOST DINOSAURS LIVED IN THE <u>JURASSIC PERIOD</u>

It's the best-known of the three Mesozoic periods, but the Jurassic wasn't the one in which most dinosaurs lived and thrived. The Cretaceous Period was when the greatest variety of dinosaur species lived.

THE SCIENCE

We know of more dinosaurs from the Late Cretaceous Period than any other. However, the numbers might not *completely* accurately reflect the numbers and variety of species that existed in the different periods. Rocks containing fossils from this period are nearer the surface than those from the Jurassic and Triassic, which means they are easier to find.

DINOSAUR COUNT
We know of more than 900 non-avian dinosaur species, which belong to more than 700 different groups.

VERDICT
Fake

FOOTPRINTS
REVEAL HOW DINOSAURS
MOVED

FACT OR FAKE?

Fossil footprints of ancient creatures tell us a lot about them. A simple shape preserved in rock might not seem like much, but clever palaeontologists can work out all sorts of information, including a dinosaur's size, weight and speed from a footprint.

THE SCIENCE

Dinosaurs in the same larger groups often had very similar feet, and so very similar footprints. That makes it hard to identify exactly which dinosaur made a print. But how deep the print is, how far apart the tracks are from each other and how well defined they are tell us a lot about how the dinosaur was moving.

VERDICT
Fact

37

CROCODILES LIVED ALONGSIDE DINOSAURS

We're old friends.

The crocodiles you see today look like prehistoric creatures – dull-coloured, scaly, covered in lumps and bumps, and with terrifying teeth that could tear you apart. This ancient appearance is probably because crocodilians are a very old group of animals.

THE SCIENCE

Like dinosaurs, crocodiles began to evolve in the Triassic Period (see page 6). The first prehistoric crocs had nostrils on the top of their heads rather than their snouts. Some of them moved around on their two back legs. They were also (surprisingly) vegetarian!

VERDICT
Fact

SURVIVORS

Crocodiles probably survived the mass extinction because they are amazingly adaptable animals. They can live in water or on land and can survive in total darkness.

DILOPHOSAURUS COULD SPIT POISON

There's a famous scene in a famous dinosaur film when a small but deadly dinosaur called *Dilophosaurus* flips out a hidden neck frill and spits poison at a baddie trying to escape. But this depiction of *Dilophosaurus* is a long way from accurate.

THE SCIENCE

To begin with, this dinosaur was much bigger – up to 4 m tall. It also had no neck frill (although it did have two upright crests on its head). But most importantly, *Dilophosaurus* could not spit poison! In fact, no known dinosaur was poisonous.

VERDICT

Fake

39

PTEROSAURS HAD FEATHERED WINGS

FACT OR FAKE?

Pterosaurs had wings (how else could they fly?) but they weren't feathered like the wings of modern birds. They were more like a bat's wings, made of skin, muscles and fibres that formed a membrane which stretched along their arms.

THE SCIENCE

Recent discoveries suggest that some of the pterosaurs might have had feathers, instead of scaly skin. But these feathers were on the body and would only have been there for warmth. Pterosaurs didn't need flight feathers.

VERDICT
Fake

THERE WERE NO FLOWERS ON EARTH WHEN THE DINOSAURS FIRST EVOLVED

FACT OR FAKE?

There were plenty of plants in prehistoric times. Ferns, pines and mosses all flourished in the Mesozoic climate, and were enjoyed by plant-eating dinosaurs. However, nature was not as colourful as it is today. Back in the early days of the dinosaurs, there were no flowers at all.

THE SCIENCE

Flowering plants began to take root on Earth about 130 million years ago, in the Cretaceous Period – the last age of the dinosaurs. This was probably due to a change in the climate, as proper seasons began to occur. So, only the last of the dinosaurs to evolve would have enjoyed the sight of flowers.

VERDICT
Fact

FIRST FLOWER
The earliest flowering plant we know about is *Archaefructus*, which had small, simple flowers. It's now extinct.

DINOSAURS AND MAMMALS LIVED AT THE SAME TIME

Has that T. rex gone?

FACT OR FAKE?

Because the Mesozoic Era is also known as the 'Age of Reptiles', it's easy to believe that other types of animal hadn't evolved yet. In fact, although reptiles were by far the most widespread group, early mammals lived alongside dinosaurs in the prehistoric world.

THE SCIENCE

Most Mesozoic mammals were little creatures, no bigger than a mouse. They fed on small insects and usually came out only at night. But there were one or two bigger and braver mammals. *Repenomamus* was about as big as a badger, with a long tail – and it even ate small dinosaurs. A *Repenomamus* fossil has been found with a young dinosaur in its stomach!

VERDICT

Fact

GRASS WAS THE MAIN FOOD FOR HERBIVOROUS DINOSAURS

FACT OR FAKE?

Do you imagine herds of herbivorous dinosaurs spending their days lazily chewing lush green grass, like modern cows? If so, your picture of plant life in the prehistoric world isn't quite right!

THE SCIENCE

Grasses didn't start properly growing until about 50 million years ago – a good 15 million years after the dinosaurs died. Before then, there was very little grass on Earth. Herbivorous dinosaurs feasted on ferns and shrubs near the ground. Long-necked herbivores stripped tender leaves from the treetops.

FANTASTIC FERNS

Ferns were one of the most widespread plants in the Mesozoic Era – and some are truly ancient. They existed on Earth long before the dinosaurs.

VERDICT

Fake

43

MOST DINOSAURS WALKED ON TIPTOE

FACT OR FAKE?

Some dinosaurs had hoof-shaped feet, while some had separate toes. Some had three claws, while others had four or even five claws. Different groups had different foot structures. But one thing most had in common was their way of walking: almost all dinosaurs travelled on their tiptoes!

THE SCIENCE

Theropods moved on their long, slender toes and sauropods were raised by a thick heel pad. This gave them a longer stride, which was useful when running. It also saved energy, because they didn't have to raise and lower the heel with every step. This might not sound like much, but when you're as heavy as a dinosaur, lifting your foot takes a lot of effort!

VERDICT

Fact

Who are you calling big-head?

TRICERATOPS HAD THE
BIGGEST SKULL
OF ANY LAND ANIMAL

FACT OR FAKE?

With its large neck frill, *Triceratops* ranks among the biggest of the big-headed dinosaurs. But the very largest skull belongs to another ceratopsid, *Pentaceratops*. The enormous neck frill made its head perhaps 3 m high – almost as tall as an African elephant!

THE SCIENCE

Although the neck frill looked solid, beneath the skin stretched over it, the bones had huge holes in them, called fenestrae. Without the holes to lighten the load, the dinosaur would hardly have been able to lift its head!

VERDICT
Fake

SOLID BONE
Triceratops was unusual among the ceratopsids because its neck frill was made of solid bone, with no fenestrae.

STEGOSAURUS

Who stole my back-up brain?!

FACT OR FAKE?

For many years, scientists speculated that armoured *Stegosaurus* had two brains: one in its head and one in its bum. A stupid suggestion? Well, we now know that it's *not* true, but the idea isn't as crazy as it might sound.

HAD TWO BRAINS

THE SCIENCE

The 'double-brain' theory came from the discovery that *Stegosaurus* and some other dinosaurs had a large hollow area in the backbones near their hips. Could this be where a second brain was located, which controlled their huge, heavy tails? Experts now think this is more likely to be something called the 'glycogen body', which stores a substance that gives the body energy. Modern birds have this feature.

BRAIN POWER

Dinosaurs *did* have small brains considering their body size (see page 15). Perhaps they'd have been smarter if they'd had this unusual 'bum-brain' after all!

VERDICT

Fake

TYRANNOSAURUS LIVED DURING THE JURASSIC PERIOD

JURASSIC PARK
Cretaceous Park

Despite what a certain film franchise might lead you to believe, *Tyrannosaurus* was not a Jurassic dinosaur. For that matter, nor were *Velociraptor*, *Triceratops*, *Gallimimus* or many other dinosaurs with a starring role in the films.

THE SCIENCE

Tyrannosaurus was a late developer – the species only evolved in the Late Cretaceous Period, around 80 million years ago. They lived in the areas that are now the USA and Canada, where more than 20 nearly complete fossil skeletons of *Tyrannosaurus* have been found.

MEET STAN

In 2020, a fossil skeleton of a *Tyrannosaurus rex*, named Stan, was sold at auction – for nearly $32 million!

VERDICT
Fake

SAUROPODS HAD LONGER NECKS THAN A GIRAFFE

FACT OR FAKE?

Of all the modern animals, giraffes have the longest necks by a long way. An adult giraffe's neck can be an impressive 1.6 m long. But the length of some sauropods' necks makes the giraffe look like a no-neck!

THE SCIENCE

It's hard to know for sure how long the necks were on particular species, but some of them were more than 10 m and *Supersaurus*'s neck may have been 15 m! They were very flexible because they were made up of lots of vertebrae – separate bones held together with strong muscles and tissue.

VERDICT
Fact

TITANOSAURS WERE THE
BIGGEST
DINOSAURS

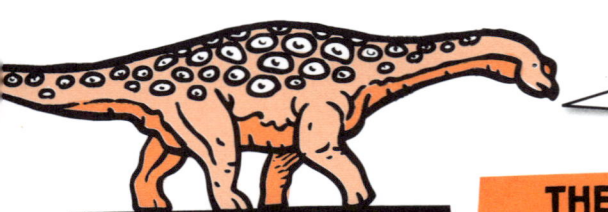

Am I too tiny to be a titanosaur?

FACT OR FAKE?

Titanosaurs were a sauropod sub-group. And as their name suggests, members of this club were some of the giants of the dinosaur world, including *Patagotitan*, *Argentinosaurus* (see pages 64–65) and *Dreadnoughtus*.

THE SCIENCE

The titanosaurs were the last group of giant herbivores to evolve, in the Late Cretaceous Period, and they were some of the biggest beasts ever to walk the Earth. However, not all the titanosaurs were giants. At just 13 m, *Saltasaurus* was only half the size of some of its titanosaur cousins!

VERDICT
Fact

BODY ARMOUR
One feature that was different from the earlier sauropods was that the titanosaurs had basic armour – tough, bony plates covering some of their body.

DINOSAURS LIVED ALONE

> We'd rather hang out in herds!

FACT OR FAKE?

Dinosaurs were a hugely diverse group of animals. They lived in different habitats, ate different things, communicated in different ways, and generally had a lifestyle that suited their different needs. This applied to their social behaviour, too. But while a few species seem to have been solitary creatures, evidence increasingly suggests that most dinosaurs lived in herds.

THE SCIENCE

We know this from tracks that show dinosaurs moving in groups to and from communal nesting sites. This is particularly likely for the many plant-eating dinosaurs. There would have been safety in numbers, where group members could protect each other from attack.

VERDICT

Fake

PTEROSAURS HAD FINGERS

Because the pterosaurs had wings, we tend to think of them as being more like birds than other animals. But they were reptiles, like the dinosaurs, and had reptilian features, including arms, hands and – yes – fingers.

THE SCIENCE

A pterosaur had three normal-size fingers, or claws, on its arm, plus a very long fourth finger. The wing membrane was attached to the reptile's shoulder and stretched along the full length of this elongated finger. The three 'normal' fingers were attached to a wrist.

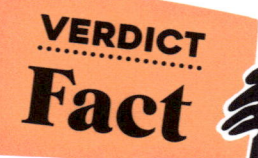

VERDICT

Fact

DINOSAURS ARE THE OLDEST ANIMAL FOSSILS EVER FOUND

FACT OR FAKE?

You can't argue with the fact that the dinosaurs lived a *very* long time ago – the earliest of them emerged about 252 million years ago. But they weren't the first life-forms on the planet by a long shot, and fossils much older than those of the dinosaurs have been discovered.

THE SCIENCE

Some of the oldest fossils belonging to land animals are those of *Kampekaris* – a kind of ancient millipede that lived 425 million years ago. Fossils of a primitive fish called *Metaspriggina* are about 505 million years old!

VERDICT

Fake

OLD FISH

Some of the very oldest fossils belonged to an odd, oval-shaped creature a bit like a jellyfish. They're about 558 million years old!

(Still) Cretaceous

Mon	Tue	Wed	Thur	Fri	Sat	Sun
X	X	X	X	X	X	X
X	X	X	X	X	X	X
X	X	X	X	X		

THE CRETACEOUS WAS THE LONGEST OF THE DINOSAUR PERIODS

FACT OR FAKE?

The third and final period of the Mesozoic Era wasn't just the longest of the three, lasting 79 million years. It was also the time when dinosaurs really flourished and there were dramatic changes on Earth.

THE SCIENCE

The Cretaceous Period came to quite a sudden end (geologically speaking) when something that scientists call the K-Pg (Cretaceous-Paleogene) extinction event occurred (see pages 90–91).

VERDICT

Fact

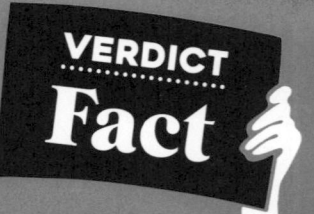

GREAT AGE

The Cretaceous Period lasted longer than the whole amount of time that's passed between the land-based dinosaurs dying out and the present day.

THEROPODS STOOD ON THEIR BACK LEGS

We think of the meat-eating theropods standing and running on their hind legs. But is that really how they moved? In this case, the popular image seem to be correct. Most theropods had fairly short arms, which they wouldn't have used for walking.

THE SCIENCE

Some dinosaurs were quadrupeds – walking on all fours. Others were bipeds, moving on their two back legs. A few species were able to do both! Some of the plant-eating dinosaurs, which moved on all four legs, could rear up on their hind legs to reach tasty leaves in the topmost branches.

VERDICT Fact

55

WE ONLY KNOW ABOUT DINOSAURS FROM FOSSIL BONES

FACT OR FAKE?

Fossil bones are important finds. They allow palaeontologists to reconstruct dinosaur skeletons, so we know how big they were, how they looked, and so on. But bones aren't the only discoveries that tell the story of the dinosaurs.

THE SCIENCE

Dinosaur eggs, some of them still in preserved nest hollows, tell us about how the dinosaurs reproduced and cared for their young. Fossil remains of the bony armour plates and spikes from armoured dinosaurs show us how they looked and protected themselves. Teeth and coprolite – that's fossilised poo to you – tell us what dinosaurs liked to eat.

LIVING RELATIVES
Of course, we also have birds, which are regarded as living dinosaur descendants, and give many clues about their extinct relatives.

VERDICT
....
Fake

SOME DINOSAURS HAD BEAKS

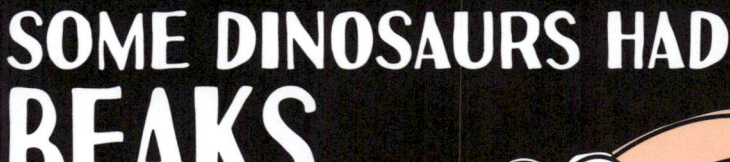

FACT OR FAKE?

We don't tend to think of dinosaurs as being beaky creatures. But since dinosaurs and birds are directly related, it shouldn't seem unusual that some dinosaurs had a beak instead of a snout or jaws filled with fangs!

Quack!

THE SCIENCE

If you look closely at dinosaurs like *Triceratops*, you'll see that they have a bony beak, a bit like a turtle's beak. This was useful for scraping up lots of leaves or vegetation in one go. The hadrosaurs, or 'duck-bills', were a whole group of dinosaurs that had flat, duck-like bills. They chewed their food with a side-to-side motion.

VERDICT

Fact

ANKYLOSAURUS COULD BREAK A TYRANNOSAURUS'S LEG WITH ITS TAIL

Don't make me angry ...

FACT OR FAKE?

Ankylosaurs were among the best-protected dinosaurs. Thanks to their thick, bony plates, scattered with knobs and spikes, there was little chance of a predator finding a soft spot to sink its teeth into. But ankylosaurs had an extra weapon in their armoury!

THE SCIENCE

At the end of their tail, these dinosaurs had a huge bony club. This thick, heavy weapon could do some serious damage. With a carefully aimed swing from its tail, *Ankylosaurus* could break the leg bones of pretty much any predator.

VERDICT

Fact

58

DINOSAURS DIDN'T HAVE EARS

Some animals have very noticeable ears. You can't miss them on an elephant or a jerboa, for example. Dinosaur ears are harder to spot, but that doesn't mean they didn't have them!

THE SCIENCE

Dinosaurs didn't have ears that stuck out; instead they had ear holes. These led to nerve canals in the skull that allowed the dinosaur to hear things. This might not sound very effective, but dinosaurs – like most other animals – probably had excellent hearing.

EAR FOSSILS?

Ears are made of cartilage and soft tissue, so they don't turn into fossils in the same way that bone does. Experts guess how dinosaurs' ears worked by looking at modern animals.

VERDICT
....
Fake

GIANT SEA TURTLES EXISTED IN DINOSAUR TIMES

Hope those dinos don't see me in here!

FACT OR FAKE?

Turtles have proved to be one of Earth's most resilient creatures. They first evolved around 230 million years ago, in the Triassic Period, and huge turtles swam in the prehistoric seas.

THE SCIENCE

While some species did die out in the extinction event that killed off the land-dwelling dinosaurs (see pages 90–91), others survived. Unusually, after this, many more turtle species evolved!

ANCIENT ARCHELON

The Cretaceous *Archelon* is the largest turtle ever to have existed, measuring more than 4.5 m from tail to snout.

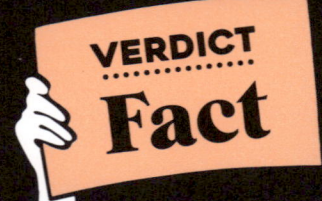

VERDICT

Fact

SAUROPODS HAD TO EAT ALMOST CONSTANTLY

FACT OR FAKE?

Imagine having to eat enough food to fuel a 10-tonne body bigger than a bus! That's the task the giant sauropods faced every day. It was tough to do when you only ate plants, which aren't high in calories.

THE SCIENCE

Large plant-eating dinosaurs would have to spend almost all their time feeding. They would graze on shrubs close to the ground, or stretch up their long necks to strip leaves from the trees. It's estimated that they would need to eat more than 1 tonne of vegetation a day just to keep their energy up!

VERDICT

Fact

SOME DINOSAURS HAD FEATHERS

We think of prehistoric dinosaurs as having thick, scaly skin, like modern reptiles. But they may not all have been like this. Scientists have found evidence that some dinosaurs may have been covered in feathers – perhaps even the terrifying *Tyrannosaurus*!

Do I look frightening in these feathers?

THE SCIENCE

Some fossils show evidence of what scientists think may have been a fluffy, feathery body covering, particularly among the theropods – the group from which birds evolved. No evidence has been found of feathers on sauropods or hadrosaurs – but that might just be because the right fossils haven't been discovered yet!

VERDICT
Fact

MEGALODON PREYED ON DINOSAURS

FACT OR FAKE?

The terrifying prehistoric shark Megalodon grew to 18 m long and weighed as much as 30 modern great white sharks. It probably would have enjoyed a hearty meal of dinosaurs if it could – but it would have needed a time machine to do so!

THE SCIENCE

Megalodon may have been prehistoric, but prehistory covers a very long time and not every ancient creature was around at the same time. Megalodon evolved more than 45 million years after the extinction of the dinosaurs!

SHARK SURVIVAL

Sharks actually evolved long before dinosaurs did. And they were one of the animal groups that lived through the mass extinction at the end of the Cretaceous Period, to survive to the present day.

VERDICT
Fake

ARGENTINOSAURUS
WAS THE
BIGGEST DINOSAUR

FACT OR FAKE?

Ask a group of palaeontologists which was the biggest dinosaur and you could find yourself in the middle of a heated debate! There are several contenders for the prize of Biggest Dinosaur Ever. At up to 40 m tall and weighing 100 tonnes, *Argentinosaurus* is undoubtedly one of them. But *Patagotitan* and some other sauropods may have been larger overall.

THE SCIENCE

It's impossible to know for sure how big any dinosaur was, and even harder to compare species. Experts can make good estimates based on the length of bones they find, but even a near-complete fossil skeleton may not accurately represent all examples of the dinosaur type.

VERDICT

Fake

(or maybe Fact!)

Hello down there!

THE MEASURE OF THINGS

The idea of how 'big' something is can also be judged in different ways. Is it how tall a dinosaur was, or how long, or how heavy — or a trickily calculated mixture of all these measurements?

MANY COMPLETE DINOSAUR FOSSILS HAVE BEEN FOUND

I'm just a lazy bones.

FACT OR FAKE?

If it was a simple process for animals to become fossils when they died, there would be fossils *everywhere*. It happens very rarely, and it's even more unusual for a complete creature to be found. Especially one the size of a dinosaur!

THE SCIENCE

The unfortunate fact is that there are almost no complete dinosaur skeletons. Some amazing finds are almost complete, but even these will be missing a few smaller bones, which have been crushed or washed away, for example.

PALAEONTOLOGIST PUZZLE

Some dinosaur species are known from just a very few bones. Palaeontologists have to work out whether these belong to a new species or one that already exists.

VERDICT

Fake

THERE WAS NO ICE AT THE NORTH POLE WHEN DINOSAURS EVOLVED

North Pole

THE SCIENCE

It's hard to imagine Earth's poles without ice – it is, after all, their defining feature. But that hasn't always been the case. When dinosaurs first emerged in the Triassic Period, which began 252 million years ago, the North and South poles were much warmer than they are today.

Earth was one big landmass in the Triassic, and the climate was different all over the globe. Fossils of cold-blooded creatures have been found in Arctic regions, and they wouldn't have been able to survive without strong sunshine. Ice only began to form at the poles around 33 million years ago.

VERDICT
Fact

SAUROPODS HAD AN EXTRA HEART

When scientists pieced together fossils from the sauropods and realised how huge they were, it posed a problem. How could one heart pump enough blood around such a vast body to keep these creatures alive? They wondered if perhaps these dinosaurs had an 'accessory' heart, to help get blood to their head.

THE SCIENCE

We now know that they didn't have an extra heart. But their bodies were cleverly adapted. They may have had springy neck bones, which acted as a kind of pump to help move blood all the way up their long necks to reach their (tiny!) brains.

VERDICT
Fake

SCIENTISTS ONCE THOUGHT *STEGOSAURUS'S* PLATES LAY FLAT

FACT OR FAKE?

When the first fossils of *Stegosaurus* were found, the large back plates had scientists a bit baffled. They decided that they must have covered the beast's back like plate armour, lying flat!

THE SCIENCE

Of course, we now know that the plates (called scutes) stood upright in two rows all down *Stegosaurus*'s back. They weren't solid bone, but instead had lots of blood vessels running through them. They may have been a way for the dinosaur to control its body temperature.

HUGE PLATES
Stegosaurus's back plates were massive – each one was about the size of a bicycle wheel!

VERDICT
Fact

QUETZALCOATLUS WAS ONE OF THE LARGEST FLYING CREATURES EVER

FACT OR FAKE?

Imagine looking up into the sky and seeing a creature flying above you with a wingspan longer than a bus. That was the size of the prehistoric *Quetzalcoatlus* – perhaps the largest creature ever to fly.

THE SCIENCE

Named after a feathered Mexican serpent god, *Quetzalcoatlus* lived in the Cretaceous Period. This massive flyer could weigh up to 250 kg and measured about 10.4 m from the tip of one wing to the tip of the other.

BIG BIRD

For comparison, the largest flying creature alive today is the wandering albatross, which has a wingspan of 3.7 m.

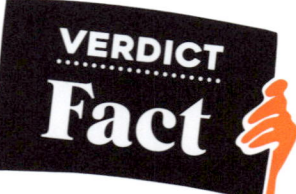

VERDICT

Fact

TYRANNOSAURUS STOOD UPRIGHT

FACT OR FAKE?

Part of the fear factor of *Tyrannosaurus* is its height – in pictures and films this dinosaur is often shown standing terrifyingly tall. But the reality is that *Tyrannosaurus* probably held itself in a horizontal posture most of the time.

THE SCIENCE

Bent forwards, with its tail straight out, the dinosaur would have been much more balanced. That means it would have been able to move and attack faster.

VERDICT

Fake

ICHTHYOSAURS WERE PREHISTORIC
FISH

FACT OR FAKE?

Ichthyosaurs looked like a mix between a dolphin and a shark. But although they lived in the water, these ancient creatures weren't fish – they were marine reptiles. They had flippers to swim quickly, and very large eyes to see in the murky ocean depths.

THE SCIENCE

Ichthyosaurs were one of several types of large, sea-dwelling reptiles that lived in the oceans of the Mesozoic world. Other fearsome sea creatures included the long-necked plesiosaurs and the fierce mosasaurs.

VERDICT
Fake

AIR-BREATHERS
Ichthyosaurs could not breathe underwater like fish. They had to come to the surface to breathe air.

SAUROPODS COULD WHIP THEIR TAILS FASTER THAN THE SPEED OF SOUND

FACT OR FAKE?

The long tails of the sauropods served several purposes. But one of the most important was as a weapon for self-defence. If it felt threatened, a sauropod could lash its tail like it was cracking a whip, with ferocious speed – and deadly effect!

THE SCIENCE

The longest sauropod tail stretched more than 12 m! They were also very flexible because they were made up of lots of vertebrae (backbones). Scientists have done tests to work out how fast these dinosaurs could flick their tails and found that it was faster than the speed of sound.

VERDICT
Fact

FOSSILS ARE PRESERVED BONES

When you see reconstructions of dinosaur skeletons in museums, they look like they're real bone, teeth, horns, and so on. But fossils aren't the dug-up bones of ancient animals. They're an imprint left in the rock.

THE SCIENCE

The soft parts of a creature's body, such as flesh and muscles, quickly decay after it dies. Hard parts, such as bone, might survive long enough to sink into the ground and be buried by rock called sediment. The bones slowly disappear and are replaced by substances called minerals. These harden and create a kind of cast of the bones' shape within the rock. That's your fossil!

VERDICT
Fake

DINOSAURS DIDN'T SMELL WELL

I smell lunch!

FACT OR FAKE?

A good sense of smell is essential for the survival of most animals, and dinosaurs were no exception. Fossil finds suggest that in some species, the part of the brain responsible for the sense of smell was bigger than normal. These dinosaurs would have had an even better sense of smell!

THE SCIENCE

Herbivorous dinosaurs would have used their good sense of smell for finding plants. It would also have helped them sense when predators were dangerously close! In the same way, carnivorous dinosaurs could sniff out their next meal. All dinosaurs probably smelt a potential mate, too.

SUPER SENSES

A dinosaur's other senses were also well developed. Most of them could see and hear with incredible accuracy.

VERDICT
Fake

ALL PTEROSAURS WALKED ON TWO LEGS LIKE BIRDS

FACT OR FAKE?

The group of large flying reptiles called pterosaurs didn't spend all their time in the air. They frequently moved around on land. Some of them did walk on two legs the way that modern birds do. But pterosaurs weren't birds, and in fact many of them travelled across land using four limbs.

THE SCIENCE

To walk like this, the pterosaur would fold up its arms and wings and use them as front limbs. It looked almost as if they were walking on their elbows at the front. It was quite a clumsy posture and they probably didn't move at high speed on the ground!

VERDICT

Fake

MOST DINOSAURS' BACK LEGS WERE LONGER THAN THEIR FRONT ONES

FACT OR FAKE?

You can clearly see that bipedal dinosaurs such as the theropods had longer, stronger back legs than front ones. What may not be so obvious is that even the dinosaurs that moved on all fours usually had longer back legs, too.

THE SCIENCE

Longer hind limbs allow an animal to run faster, because they have more power to push off from the ground. Having smaller front limbs reduces their overall weight and improves their balance.

UNUSUAL ARMS

Brachiosaurus was an unusual dinosaur because its front legs were longer than its back ones. That's how it earned its name: 'arm lizard'!

VERDICT
Fact

TYRANNOSAURUS

Slow down!

FACT OR FAKE?

If you had to escape from a *Tyrannosaurus*, what would be the best tactic? Punch it on the nose like a shark? Shout at it like a wolf? Instinct would probably simply say RUN! But if you did, what are your chances of survival? Just how fast was a *Tyrannosaurus*?

VERDICT

Fake

COULD OUTRUN A CAR

THE SCIENCE

The fact is that the big *T. rex* probably wasn't super speedy. Experts reckon the dinosaur's top speed was about 27 kph. If you had a car handy, you could easily escape a grisly death by jumping in and putting your foot down.

ON FOOT

The fastest man in the world, Usain Bolt, can sprint at more than 44 kph – no danger of being caught by a *Tyrannosaurus*.

DINOSAURS COULD LIVE TO BE 150 YEARS OLD

FACT OR FAKE?

Big animals usually live longer than smaller ones. Just compare an elephant, which lives an average 60 years, to a mouse, which has a life expectancy of just a year! So, dinosaurs *did* live long lives – but not into their hundreds!

THE SCIENCE

It's tough to tell how old dinosaurs were when they died. Sometimes rings in the fossil bones give us a hint, like the rings inside tree trunks. But usually there's little evidence. However, comparing certain species to what we know about modern animals has led to estimates of about 80 years for a sauropod.

VERDICT
Fake

DOME-HEADED DINOSAURS USED THE DOMES FOR FIGHTING

Come at me, bro!

FACT OR FAKE?

Like many unusual dinosaur features, the large bony skulls of the pachycephalosaurs had scientists scratching their own heads. What was the purpose of having such a thick skull? They assumed that it must be for fighting – when two pachycephalosaurs fought, they cracked skulls!

THE SCIENCE

This was a reasonable assumption, but later logic suggests that might not be the case. The domes on these dinosaurs' heads were solid – there was nothing to absorb the blow of a head-on-head butt, so it would have hurt or even injured the dinosaur.

THE MYSTERY REMAINS

Scientists still don't know for sure what the domes were for. They may have been a way to attract a mate – or simply to look impressive or scary!

VERDICT

Fake

DINOSAURS USED THEIR TAILS FOR BALANCE

The downward dino.

FACT OR FAKE?

Dinosaurs' great long tails may seem like an inconvenience to carry around, but they evolved this way for a good reason. Most dinosaurs had a forward-leaning posture, carrying a lot of weight over their hips. The tails were probably used to balance the front and back ends of a dinosaur's body.

THE SCIENCE

On some dinosaurs, the tail was the same length as their body to create a perfect counterbalance. But the tail had other uses too – it could be a powerful weapon (see pages 58 and 73)!

VERDICT
Fact

LONGEST TAIL
Diplodocus had the longest tail of any known dinosaur. This enormous appendage could be more than 12 m long!

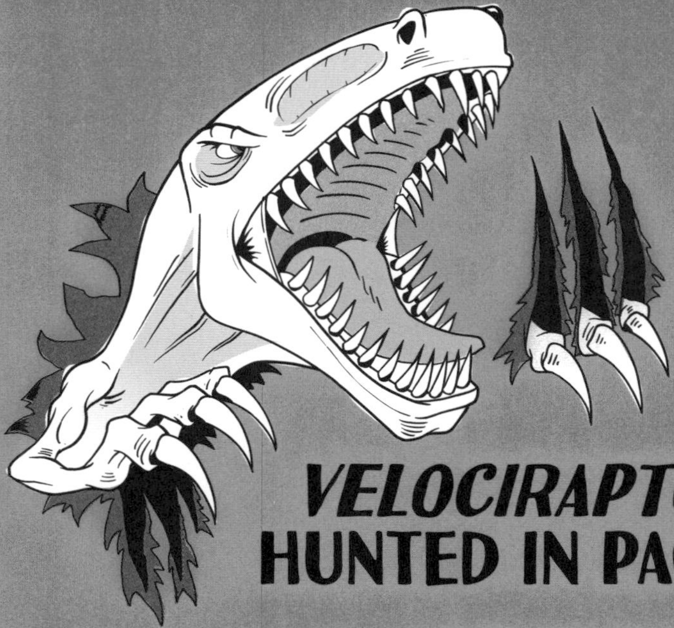

VELOCIRAPTOR HUNTED IN PACKS

FACT OR FAKE?

There is evidence that some dinosaurs did hunt down prey in packs, working together to bring down an unsuspecting herbivore to make a good meal for the pack to share. But evidence suggests that this isn't how *Velociraptor* hunted.

THE SCIENCE

Fossil evidence doesn't tell us how dinosaurs hunted, of course. But experts can make good guesses based on what they can work out from their diet, their teeth, and by looking at similar modern animals. It seems more likely that while several *Velociraptor* may have targeted the same prey, they did not co-operate with each other. Every dinosaur for itself!

VERDICT
Fake

83

THE NAME 'RAPTOR' MEANS 'ATTACKER'

Mine!

FACT OR FAKE?

Velociraptor ... *Microraptor* ... *Bambiraptor* ... the raptors were small, carnivorous theropods. Species such as *Velociraptor* have a reputation for being vicious attackers, but that's not what the 'raptor' part of their name means.

THE SCIENCE

Raptor means 'thief' or 'plunderer'. *Oviraptor* got its name 'egg thief' because the first fossil was found near a nest of eggs it was thought to be stealing. It was later found to be the *Oviraptor*'s own nest!

VERDICT
Fake

MODERN RAPTORS
Raptors still exist! Modern birds of prey that hunt from the air are known as raptors.

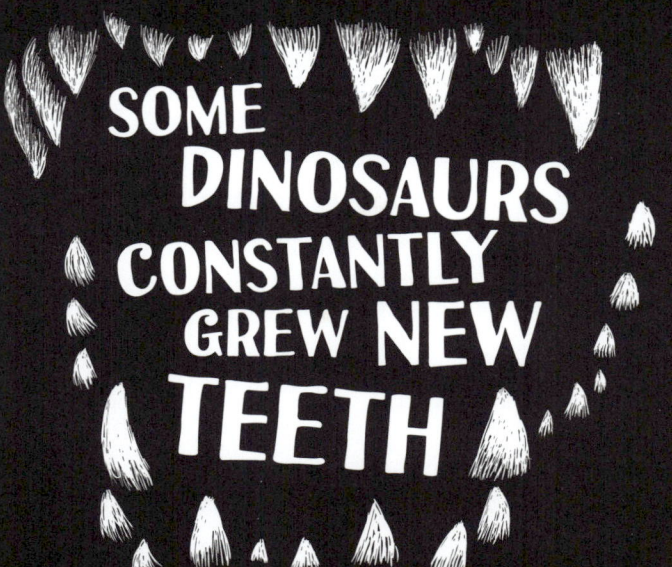

SOME DINOSAURS CONSTANTLY GREW NEW TEETH

FACT OR FAKE?

Dinosaurs ate a lot – and their diets weren't dainty. Tearing at flesh and constantly chewing tough plant matter took a toll on their teeth. But a dinosaur wouldn't survive long if its teeth wore down or fell out, so nature found a solution.

THE SCIENCE

Many dinosaurs grew teeth in a kind of conveyor-belt system! New teeth would grow in rows at the back of the jaw, and move forwards to replace teeth that were broken or worn out. Sometimes a dinosaur might have a whole new set of gnashers every few weeks!

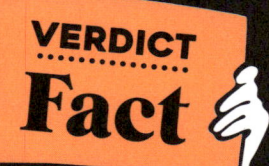

VERDICT

Fact

SEISMOSAURUS CHOKED TO DEATH

FACT OR FAKE?

Only one fossil example of giant *Seismosaurus* has ever been found. But it revealed some interesting information. It showed that this was a huge dinosaur – perhaps up to 50 m long, with a neck of 21 m! It also suggested how this giant met its end.

THE SCIENCE

Scientists found a stone lodged in the dinosaur's throat. They believe it may have swallowed this gastrolith (see page 29) and choked to death when it got stuck. But there's another possible explanation. A large *Allosaurus* tooth was also found on the fossil site. So perhaps *Seismosaurus* was attacked and killed by a predator.

IS IT REAL?

The unlucky *Seismosaurus* may not be its own species. Some scientists think these fossil remains may be a type of *Diplodocus*.

VERDICT
Fact
(or Fake?)

TYRANNOSAURUS HUNTED *STEGOSAURUS*

FACT OR FAKE?

We like to imagine all our favourite dinosaurs living in the same landscape at the same time. But the fact is, different dinosaur species were separated not just by geography, but by time, too.

THE SCIENCE

Stegosaurus lived in the Late Jurassic Period, around 150 million years ago. *Tyrannosaurus* lived in the Late Cretaceous Period, about 72 million years ago. *Stegosaurus* – and all the stegosaurs – had been extinct for 66 million years before *Tyrannosaurus* began its reign!

VERDICT

Fake

Hi there …

PARASAUROLOPHUS USED ITS HEAD CREST TO COMMUNICATE

Parasaurolophus belonged to the strange-looking family of hadrosaur dinosaurs. This dinosaur was known for its amazing head crest, sticking out of the back of its skull. Scientists long debated what dinosaurs like this used the crest for, but they're now pretty sure it was used to 'speak' to others of its species!

THE SCIENCE

They reached this conclusion after the discovery of a well-preserved crest. The inside of it was a bit like a musical instrument called a crumhorn. There was a chamber inside that would have echoed and amplified sounds.

VERDICT

Fact

NEW DINOSAUR SPECIES ARE BEING DISCOVERED ALL THE TIME

FACT OR FAKE?

At the moment, we know of more than 900 different species of dinosaur. That's a lot – but there may be hundreds more still to be discovered. Palaeontologists are uncovering new fossils all the time.

THE SCIENCE

Every fossil find is important. Usually, fossils belong to a species that is already known, but every new bone adds another piece to the jigsaw. Occasionally a fossil is found that doesn't fit an existing species, and a whole new dinosaur is discovered.

NEW TITAN

In April 2021 a new type of Cretaceous titanosaur (see page 50) was discovered in Chile. It was named *Arackar Licanantay*.

VERDICT
Fact

THE **DINOSAURS** WERE

People have come up with many ideas to explain why non-avian dinosaurs died out 66 million years ago. These theories include dwindling food supplies, vicious volcanic eruptions and climate change. But most experts today agree that a huge asteroid impact is the most likely cause of this mass extinction.

ARGH!

WIPED OUT BY AN ASTEROID STRIKE

It wasn't the asteroid itself that wiped out the dinosaurs, but the effect it had. The massive impact threw up huge amounts of debris. Sunlight was blocked out and for years, the sky was filled with dust. This caused such a change to the environment that most living things could not survive. As plants and small creatures began to die out, the larger dinosaurs that fed on them also went extinct.

EXTINCTION EVENT

Scientists call things like this an 'extinction event'. They've happened several times in Earth's history, but this one was particularly dramatic – three-quarters of all species of animals and plants died out.

VERDICT

Fact

GLOSSARY

adaptable – able to change to meet new conditions

asteroid – a rocky space body

biped – an animal that walks on two legs

carnivore – an animal that eats other animals

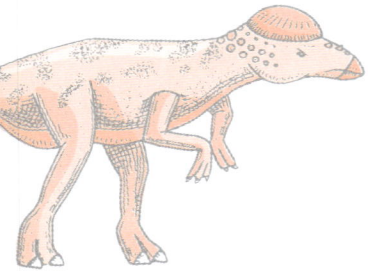

classify – to group things by particular characteristics

communal – describing things that are shared between a social group

continent – one of Earth's seven large landmasses

crest – a feature on an animal's head that can be made of fur, skin or feathers

crumhorn – a wind instrument made up of cylindrical tube with a curved end

descendant – an animal or person that lives after and is related to another animal or person that lived in the past

digestion – the process of breaking up food as it passes through the body

diverse – varied, or having lots of different types or forms

dwindling – slowly getting smaller

evolve – to change over time, such as when living things change to become more suited to their environment

extinction – when an animal or plant dies out completely, so no more of the species exist

fossil – the remains of an ancient animal preserved in rock

gastrolith – a small stone swallowed by birds and some reptiles to aid digestion

genus (plural: genera) – a large group of closely related animals or plants; there may be several different species in a genus

herbivore – an animal that only eats plants and other vegetation

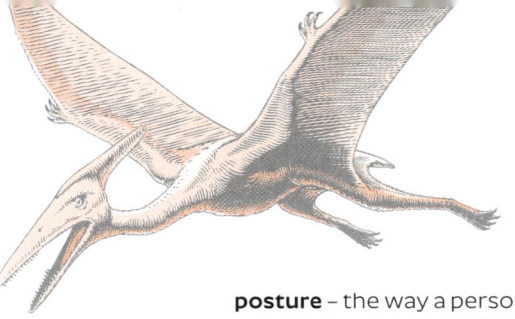

juvenile – a young example of a species, that is not yet fully grown

landmass – a large body of land, such as a continent

lush – describing something that grows well and healthily

mammal – a group of animals that have four legs and a backbone, and which give birth to live young; mammals are said to be 'warm-blooded'

membrane – a very thin layer of body tissue that acts as a barrier or lining

mineral – a solid substance that occurs naturally on Earth

nurture – to feed, protect and take care of something

omnivore – an animal that has a diet that includes both meat and plants

palaeontologist – a scientist who studies the ancient remains of once-living things

pigment – colour

posture – the way a person or animal stands or holds itself – the position of its body

predator – an animal that hunts other animals for food

quadruped – an animal that walks on all fours

reconstructions – versions of something, such as animal skeletons, that have been recreated to look as they would have done in ancient times

reptile – a group of animals that have four legs, a backbone and which usually lay eggs; reptiles are usually considered 'cold-blooded'

reptilian – describing things that are characteristic of reptiles

GLOSSARY

resilient – able to survive despite difficult conditions

sauropods – a group of huge, plant-eating dinosaurs characterised by their large bodies, long necks and tails, and small heads

scute – a type of bony plate found on armoured dinosaurs, such as *Stegosaurus*

sediment – small particles of rocks, minerals and other substances that are moved from one place to another by natural processes

species – a group of living things that share similar characteristics and can breed with each other

swamp – an area of low-lying land covered in water

theropods – a group of meat-eating dinosaurs that usually walked on two legs

thrive – to do well

wingspan – the length of a flying creature's wings, from the tip of one wing to the tip of the other

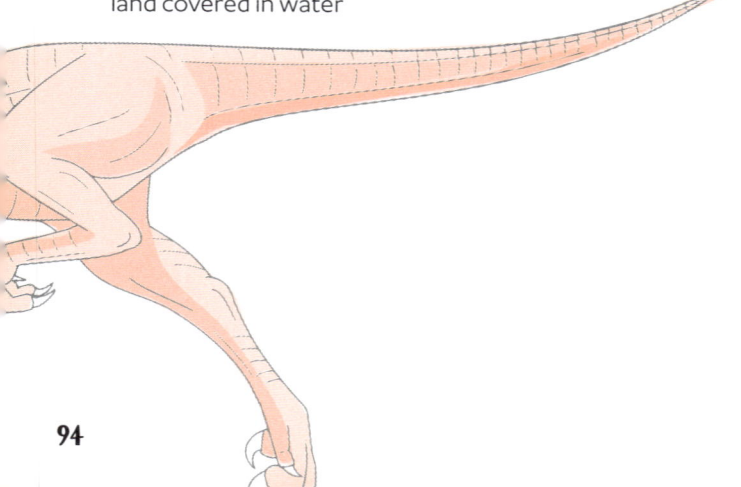

FURTHER INFORMATION

BOOKS

Dinosaur Infosaurus
by Katie Woolley (Wayland, 2021)

Dino-Sorted series
by Sonya Newland (Frankin Watts, 2021)

Dinosaurs (Go Quiz Yourself!)
by Izzi Howell (Wayland, 2020)

Dinosaurs (Prehistoric Life)
by Clare Hibbert (Franklin Watts, 2019)

WEBSITES

kids.nationalgeographic.com/animals/prehistoric
Explore the world of dinosaurs with these National
Geographic fact files.

**www.nhm.ac.uk/visit/galleries-and-museum-map/
dinosaurs.html**
Find out all about dinosaurs at the Natural History
Museum website.

www.amnh.org/dinosaurs
Take a journey through the world of the dinosaurs with loads
of articles from the American Museum of Natural History.

INDEX